everyday
calm

everyday calm

---

365 WAYS TO A TRANQUIL LIFE

An Hachette UK Company
www.hachette.co.uk

First published in 2019 by Pyramid,
an imprint of Octopus Publishing Group Ltd
Carmelite House
50 Victoria Embankment
London, EC4Y 0DZ
www.octopusbooks.co.uk

ISBN: 978-0-7537-3353-0

A CIP catalogue record for this book is
available from the British Library

Printed and bound in China

10 9 8 7 6 5 4 3 2 1

Publisher: Lucy Pessell
Designer: Lisa Layton
Design: Ummagumma
Editor: Sarah Vaughan
Contributing Editor: Emma Hill
Assistant Production Manager: Lucy Carter
Images: Shutterstock/Irtsya

INTRODUCTION

Calm (adjective):
Not showing or feeling nervousness, anger, or other strong emotions.

Calm (verb):
Make (someone) tranquil and quiet; soothe.

"They experienced calm after the storm passed."

The frenetic pace of modern life may not be conducive to cultivating a calm mindset, yet it is precisely this inner calm that will equip us to deal with our life, no matter what challenges it presents. Each of us has the power to connect to our true selves, to retreat into silence and find serenity in even the stormiest of times. Our circumstances are often beyond our control, but our reaction to them is very much within our grasp. We can choose calm in the most stressful of situations. We can find stillness in amongst the chaos.

Everyday Calm brings you ideas on how to cultivate calm daily, through acceptance, a change of pace, releasing tension, finding perspective, and spiraling inward to a place of tranquility. Here you'll find a new exercise, tip, or inspirational quote for every day of the year to help you breeze through the daily grind with grace and ease.

Don't let another year slip through your fingers in a haze of rushing, worrying, striving, and stressing. Use this book as your guide, inspiration, and motivation to let go of those emotions that no longer serve you, to slow down, simplify, appreciate, and to find a place of peace within—one day at a time—until calm becomes a way of life.

"He who lives in harmony
with himself lives in
harmony with
the universe."

– MARCUS AURELIUS

"The body benefits from movement, and the mind benefits from stillness."

– SAKYONG MIPHAM

COMMIT TO YOGA

Immersing yourself fully is the best way to reap the benefits of this wonderful, calming, and life-enhancing practice. So instead of signing up to weekly classes, commit to practicing yoga at home for 30 days in a row. Just 20 minutes a day will go a long way toward honing your skill, making yoga a habit and a way of life. There are many free 30-day programs on YouTube.

"Yoga is bringing suppleness in body, calmness in mind, kindness in heart, and awareness in life."

– AMIT RAY

"The best cure for the body is a quiet mind."

– NAPOLEON BONAPARTE

"Calmness is a huge gift. And once you master it, you will be able to respond in a useful way to every difficult situation that decides to walk into your heart."

– GERI LARKIN

ACCEPT YOUR FEELINGS

If something is causing you distress or making you angry, however it is disrupting your inner calm, don't avoid the emotion. Try to get in touch with the feelings, not in a confrontational way but rather just to acknowledge and accept them. Note that the emotion is transient and will pass.

"If it comes, let it come. If it goes, it's ok, let it go. Let things come and go. Stay calm, don't let anything disturb your peace, and carry on."

– GERMANY KENT

"True peace is a quality you carry within yourself, regardless of external circumstances."

– JOHN TEMPLETON

"Serenity comes when you trade expectations for acceptance."

– BUDDHA

RETAIN PERSPECTIVE

Don't add unnecessary stress to everyday ordeals, most of which are trivial. Unless it's a life-or-death situation, remind yourself that it really doesn't matter that much.

"You cannot wait
for an untroubled
world to have
an untroubled
moment."

– LEMONY SNICKET

WIND DOWN WITH SOME MELLOW MUSIC

Research suggests that your brain waves will sync up with the slow rhythm of the soothing music, putting you in a meditative state.

"Just slow down. Slow down your speech. Slow down your breathing. Slow down your walking. Slow down your eating. And let this slower, steadier pace perfume your mind. Just slow down."

– DOKO

"Be still like a mountain and flow like a great river."

– LAOZI

DON'T
OVER-SCHEDULE

Inner peace can only be achieved when you're fully present in the moment. Over-stretching yourself means you will spend every day frantic and preoccupied, worried about the next place you have to be and the next thing you need to be doing.

"Savor a slow-paced contented life."

– FENNEL HUDSON

"The mind is like water. When it's turbulent, it's difficult to see. When it's calm, everything becomes clear."

– PRASAD MAHES

BE GRATEFUL

Practice gratitude as a way to calmly accept your life as it is right now. Engage in the daily habit of listing all the things you are grateful for instead of focusing on what you want and don't have.

"Calmness is the lake of the mind, thankfulness is the lake of the heart."

– UNKNOWN

"Possession of material riches, without inner peace, is like dying of thirst while bathing in a lake."

– PARAMAHANSA YOGANANDA

"Being still does not mean don't move. It means move in peace."

– E'YEN A. GARDNER

LET GO

Release yourself from the grasp of toxic relationships. You will never find inner harmony if you engage in destructive relationships.

"If you let go a little, you will have a little peace. If you let go a lot, you will have a lot of peace. If you let go completely, you will have complete peace."

– AJAHN CHAH

VISUALIZE

A visualizing meditation can be wonderful way
to cultivate calm:

1. Close your eyes and imagine yourself in a comforting
place where you can fully relax.

2. Really notice how it feels in this safe place. What can you
see? What can you hear? What you can smell?

3. Stay in your calm place for a while until you are
ready to open your eyes.

4. Reflect on how this meditation has made you feel.

Bring to mind this visualization to recapture this feeling of
serenity whenever you need to find peace.

"Meditation is such a wonderful way to calm the ocean inside us."

– DEBASISH MRIDHA MD

LIMIT DISTRACTIONS

Try to spend some time every day away from technology. Shut down your computer and leave your phone in another room, even if just for one hour a day.

"I think 99 times and find nothing. I stop thinking, swim in silence, and the truth comes to me."

– ALBERT EINSTEIN

"The greater the level of calmness of our mind, the greater our peace of mind, the greater our ability to enjoy a happy and joyful life."

– DALAI LAMA

CREATE A ZEN ZONE

Set up a haven of calm in a cozy corner of your house.
A favorite chair, soft cushions, and low lighting or candles
should feature. Take yourself there whenever you need to
find a moment of peace.

"Breathe in deeply to bring your mind home to your body."

– THICH NHAT HANH

"Silence isn't empty,
it's full of answers."

– UNKNOWN

"Only when one is connected to one's own core is one connected to others, I am beginning to discover. And, for me, the core, the inner spring, can best be found through solitude."

– ANNE MORROW LINDBERGH

FEBRUARY 3RD

SPEND TIME ALONE

Take some time alone to recharge and regroup. Without the influence of others around you it is easier to find your own equilibrium and true inner peace.

"It is very healthy to spend time alone. You need to know how to be alone and not defined by another person."

– OSCAR WILDE

"Let the mind calm down
and the heart start to open.
Then everything will be
very obvious."

— SRI SRI RAVI SHANKAR

FIND WORK YOU ENJOY

If you are in a job you don't enjoy, do all you can to find another. Explore what's out there and how you could become involved in things that truly speak to you. If you can find work that you love, you will be far more at peace with yourself.

"Learn to be quiet enough to hear the sound of the genuine within yourself so that you can hear it in others."

– MARIAN WRIGHT EDELMAN

"If you're happy in what you're doing, you'll like yourself, you'll have inner peace. And if you have that, along with physical health, you'll have more success than you could possibly have imagined."

– ROGER CARAS

"Breath is the power behind all things. I breathe in and know that good things will happen."

– TAO PORCHON-LYNCH

PRACTICE *NADI SHODHANA*

Practice the powerful technique of *Nadi Shodhana*, or alternate nostril breathing, to soothe an anxious mind:

1. Sit up tall in *sukhasana* (cross legged).
2. Relax your left hand on your lap and bring your right hand up to your face. Close your right nostril with your right thumb and inhale through the left nostril slowly and steadily.
3. Pause at the top and retain your breath for a count of two.
4. Switch sides so your index finger now seals the left nostril and exhale slowly through your right nostril.
5. Pause briefly at the bottom and then inhale deeply through the right nostril.
6. Pause at the top and retain your breath for a count of two.
7. Switch sides so your thumb now seals the right nostril and exhale slowly through your left nostril.
8. Repeat the cycle above 5–10 times.

"Feelings come and go
like clouds in a windy sky.
Conscious breathing
is my anchor."

– THICH NHAT HANH

GO FOR A GENTLE SWIM

Swimming is a particularly good way to relax the body and soothe the mind. Instead of powering on through the water, consider swimming slowly as a more restorative practice, letting the water hold and soothe you.

"Gentleness is strength under control. It is the ability to stay calm, no matter what happens."

– ELIZABETH GEORGE

GET ORGANIZED

Many stressful situations are avoidable if you prepare
ahead of time.

"Come from a place of
peace and you'll find you
can deal with anything."

– MICHAEL SINGER

"Authenticity is the daily practice of letting go of who we think we're supposed to be and embracing who we are."

– BRENË BROWN

BE KIND TO YOURSELF

Wrap your arms around yourself and give yourself a hug. You have everything you need within.

"You are worthy of every drop
of sweetness and ease that
you encounter."

– ALEX ELLE

"What is pertinent is the calmness of beauty, its sense of restraint. It is as though the land knows of its own beauty, its own greatness, and feels no need to shout it."

– KAZUO ISHIGURO

CONNECT WITH NATURE

Find a quiet place free from the mental noise that fills our everyday lives. Even in the city, you can look up at the sky, find a green space, feel the wind on your face…

"Look at a tree, a flower, a plant. Let your awareness rest upon it. How still they are, how deeply rooted in being. Allow nature to teach you stillness."

– ECKHART TOLLE

LEAVE THE PAST BEHIND

So many of the stresses and worries that ruin our sense of calm are rooted firmly in the past. Stop indulging in negative ruminations of events that have already happened and concentrate on today.

"Let go of the battle, breathe quietly and let it be."

– JACK KORNFIELD

"Your calm mind is your ultimate weapon against your challenges. So relax."

— BRYANT MCGILL

MASSAGE YOUR HANDS

For a quick massage on the go, try massaging your hands. We hold a lot of our tension here so releasing this is a simple route to feeling more relaxed.

"Within you there is a stillness and a sanctuary to which you can retreat at any time and be yourself."

– HERMANN HESSE

RECITE CALMING MANTRAS

Write some calming mantras that you can call upon in times of stress. For example, "I can handle this situation calmly and with good grace." Close and your eyes and repeat the mantra to yourself whenever needed.

"Don't feel lonely; the entire
universe is inside you."

– RUMI

"See what happens when you tune your pace to the trickle of a stream, or the waft of a lazy breeze."

– UNKNOWN

"Sometimes, it is necessary to quiet the mind in order to be able to hear. How can we tune into what is going on outside of ourselves, if it is drowned out by what is going on inside of ourselves? Find your stillness, find your calm, and listen."

– AKIROQ BROST

FIND YOUR CALM PLACE

You don't have to travel anywhere to do this, simply bring to mind a place—either real or imagined—that engenders feelings of peace. Consider drawing or writing about your "calm place" in order to make it more real and therefore reachable in times of turmoil.

"Rushing into action,
you fail. Trying to grasp
things, you lose them."

– LAOZI

"Be calm like a calm lake, then you will look beautiful like a beautiful calm lake!"

– MEHMET MURAT ILDAN

DON'T PUT PRESSURE ON YOURSELF

You don't need to be the best at everything—earning a high salary, getting straight As, being the best friend, the best mother, first over the line at everything. Find true inner calm by accepting yourself wherever you're at today.

"Listen to the sound of the
waves within you."

– RUMI

"Sometimes the most urgent and vital thing you can possibly do is take a complete rest."

– ASHLEIGH BRILLIANT

"Peace is its
own reward."

– MAHATMA GANDHI

GET CREATIVE

There is a proven relationship between getting hands-on creative—whether cooking, painting, knitting, sketching, sculpting or sewing—and relaxation. Studies have shown that indulging in such creative hobbies lowers the heart rate and blood pressure, actively calming the nervous system.

"When things get really
bad, just raise your glass and
stamp your feet and do
a little jig. That's about
all you can do."

– LEONARD COHEN

"There is a calmness to
a life lived in gratitude,
a quiet joy."

– RALPH H. BLUM

MAKE TIME FOR YOUR FRIENDS

Spending time with loved ones increases our levels of the feel-good hormone oxytocin, plus there's nothing more calming than talking worries through with good friends.

"Peace. It does not mean to be in a place where there is no noise, trouble or hard work. It means to be in the midst of those things and still be calm in your heart."

– UNKNOWN

"Maybe if we just lay beneath the stars long enough, all our worries will dissipate into the cosmos. And we can lay there motionless, yet sailing across the stars."

— TREVOR DRIGGERS

PREP FOR BED

Lack of sleep has all kinds of negative impacts of our health and well-being. It's pretty impossible to find inner peace and remain calm in difficult situations when you're feeling frazzled, so put some effort into getting a good night's sleep. Make your bedroom a comfortable, calm haven with plenty of clear space. Try and stick to the same calming bedtime routine every night—simple rituals such as having a bath or reading a book can become signifiers to your brain to relax.

"Within each of us, there is silence. A silence as vast as the universe. And when we experience that silence, we remember who we are."

– GUNILLA NORRIS

"Quiet mind,
quiet soul."

– LAILAH GIFTY AKITA

PRACTICE COMPASSION

Inner peace is difficult to attain if you are constantly focused on yourself and your own worries. When you make the time to care for others you become a more positive and peaceful person.

"Compassion, tolerance, forgiveness, and a sense of self-discipline are qualities that help us lead our daily lives with a calm mind."

– DALAI LAMA

"Don't explain your philosophy. Embody it."

– EPICTETUS

SEEK OUT THE BRIGHT SIDE

Practice optimism wherever possible. Turn negatives into positives and find a reason to smile—there is always at least one!

"Our worst
misfortunes never
happen, and most
miseries lie in
anticipation."

– HONORÉ DE BALZAC

BE EARLY

Plan to arrive everywhere 10 minutes early and say goodbye to frantic rushing and sweat-inducing commutes.

"Eat, sleep, eat. Exist slowly, softly, like these trees, like a puddle of water."

– JEAN-PAUL SARTRE

"The ideal of calm exists in a sitting cat."

– JULES RENARD

PLAY WITH A PET

Studies have shown that interacting with animals can
ease tension and promote peace of mind.

"Anxiety's like a rocking chair.
It gives you something to do,
but it doesn't get you very far."

– JODI PICOULT

"Happy is the person who can keep a quiet heart, in the chaos and tumult of this modern world."

– PATIENCE STRONG

WORRY LESS

Worrying won't change the outcome of any event, but it will take away your peace of mind today. Each time you find yourself worrying about something, try to replace that worry with a positive thought about that person or event.

"Surrender to what is. Let go of what was. Have faith in what will be."

– SONIA RICOTTI

"If the ocean can calm itself, so can you. We are both salt water mixed with air."

– NAYYIRAH WAHEED

"Be the calm eye of the storm where nothing phases you, focus on your center to remain balanced, let your life flow like a stream of wind."

– JAY WOODMAN

USE YOUR IMAGINATION

Conjure calming imagery in tricky or stressful situations. Whether it be a serene scene in nature, a beloved pet, or a vision of yourself with wings flying far above the storm…

"In the silence behind
what can be heard lies
the answers we have
been searching for
so long."

– ANDREAS FRANSSON

TUNE IN

Choose a day to rise with the sun, eat when you're hungry, drink when you're thirsty, and sleep when you're tired. This can be a wonderful way of tuning in to your body's natural rhythms and finding an inner calm that is hard to attain within the usual daily structure of alarm clocks and deadlines.

"Never be in a hurry; do everything quietly and in a calm spirit. Do not lose your inner peace for anything whatsoever, even if your whole world seems upset."

– ST. FRANCIS DE SALES

STOP

There is always time to stop for just a moment. To check in with yourself, to take a few deep calming breaths, and just to notice.

"There are times when we stop, we sit still. We listen and breezes from a whole other world begin to whisper."

– JAMES CARROLL

"Stillness reveals the secrets of eternity."

– LAOZI

SEE THE BIGGER PICTURE

When we're stressed or frustrated it's often because we are unable to step out from our own limited viewpoint and see the bigger picture—to understand where others are coming from and put it all in perspective. Try to step outside of yourself today and take a bird's-eye view of any stressful situation. Gaining true perspective is incredibly calming.

"Rule number one is, don't sweat the small stuff. Rule number two is, it's all small stuff."

– ROBERT ELIOT

"Anxiety does not empty tomorrow of its sorrows, but only empties today of its strength."

– CHARLES SPURGEON

"When everything seems crazy, you be the calm. Don't let the chaos you are facing inside of you."

– BRYANT MCGILL

TIE UP LOOSE ENDS

Leave nothing unresolved in your life and inner peace will be far easier to achieve. Regret the way you left things with an old friend? Get in touch and tell them as much. Maybe you have an argument hanging over your head? Call the person you've argued with and talk it through.

"If you want to fly,
give up everything that
weighs you down."

– UNKNOWN

PRACTICE PATIENCE

Practice being patient as a way to stay calm in times of stress. You can do this every day in many small ways—don't automatically opt for the smallest queue in the supermarket, or the traffic-free route with no hold-ups. Instead, choose to put yourself in these more frustrating situations, and choose to stay calm.

"One minute of patience,
ten years of peace."

– GREEK PROVERB

"Look at a tree, how calm, lovely and beautiful she is. She is always meditating for the love of the sun."

– DEBASISH MRIDHA MD

STEP OUTSIDE

If you spend much of your working day indoors, make an effort
to step outside on your lunch break. Leave your to-do list behind
and let the fresh air clear your head. If possible, walk to a green
space such as a park or public garden and let the soothing
qualities of your surrounds wash over you.

"Mother nature has the power to please, to comfort, to calm, and to nurture one's soul."

– ANTHONY DOUGLAS WILLIAMS

USE LAVENDER OIL

Research has shown that inhaling certain scents, such as
lavender, can help calm bodily systems.

"The time to relax is when you don't have time for it."

— SYDNEY J. HARRIS

NOTICE YOUR REACTION

Focus on your senses when you're feeling wound up or stressed. Notice how your palms are sweaty, or your heart is beating faster. Don't judge these reactions, just calmly acknowledge them and your body will switch out of its automatic stress response far more quickly.

"By staying calm, you increase your resistance against any kind of storms."

– MEHMET MURAT ILDAN

"Learn to calm down the winds of your mind, and you will enjoy great inner peace."

– REMEZ SASSON

"Live the actual
moment. Only this
actual moment is life."

– THICH NHAT HANH

ACCEPT

Accept what is and stop struggling against it.

"Be patient and calm; no one can catch fish in anger."

— HERBERT HOOVER

"Be where you are, not where you think you should be."

– UNKNOWN

"Being relaxed, at peace with yourself, confident, emotionally neutral, loose, and free-floating—these are the keys to successful performance in almost everything."

– WAYNE W. DYER

"The ocean doesn't complain about the dance of ten million waves; so don't be concerned with the rise and fall of thoughts."

– PAPAJI

"This, too, shall pass."

— ATTAR OF NISHAPUR

BREATHE

When you're feeling stressed, breathe. Use the breath as the powerful tool it is in countering the body's natural response to stress by taking the following steps:

1. Close your eyes, place your hands on your lower ribcage, and take a deep breath in. Feel your breath traveling downward and the expansion of your belly against your hands as you inhale deeply.

2. Exhale slowly and fully until all the air has exited your lungs, imagining all the stress leaving your body as you do so.

3. Repeat steps 1. and 2. five times.

4. Smile.

"Breath is the power behind all things...I breathe in and know that good things will happen."

– TAO PORCHON-LYNCH

"You can't calm the storm so stop trying. What you can do is calm yourself. The storm will pass."

– TIMBER HAWKEYE

GET A GRIP

When you next find yourself stressing over an issue, ask yourself will this matter next week, next month, next year, in 5 years…? The answer, more often than not, will be a resounding no.

"Sometimes people let the same problem make them miserable for years when they could just say, 'So what.' That's one of my favorite things to say. 'So what.'"

– ANDY WARHOL

"Set peace of mind
as your highest goal,
and organize your life
around it."

– BRIAN TRACY

PRIORITIZE

So you have hundreds of things to do, and no time to do them all. Step back and prioritize. What really needs to be done today and what can wait until tomorrow? You'll be surprised at how much of your to-do list falls into the latter category and just how much "stuff" you're unnecessarily fretting about.

"Patience is the calm acceptance that things can happen in a different order than the one you have in mind."

– DAVID G. ALLEN

"The stiller you are, the calmer life is."

– RASHEED OGUNLARU

HAVE A PAJAMA DAY

Take a day to completely withdraw and wind down. Stay in your pajamas, cozy up on the couch, and shut out the hustle of the outside world.

"Take rest. A field
that has rested gives
bountiful crops."

– OVID

"Let us accept the invitation, ever-open, from the Stillness, taste its exquisite sweetness, and heed its silent instruction."

– PAUL BRUNTON

MAKE A BIG TASK SMALL

If it's a seemingly insurmountable task that's disrupting your inner calm, break it down into smaller manageable tasks, which will instantly make it feel more achievable. Take one small step at a time and you'll soon find yourself at the top of the mountain.

"It's the steady, quiet,
plodding ones who win
in the lifelong race."

– ROBERT W. SERVICE

"When problems come, remain calm in two cases. One when you know you can solve them so smile; second, when you know you can't so be silent."

– VIKRMN

"You find peace
by coming to terms
with what you
don't know."

– NASSIM NICHOLAS TALEB

BE FLEXIBLE

No matter how carefully we plan, things will always crop up unexpectedly. Always prepare to be flexible and adapt to changing situations so your body's stress responses are not automatically triggered when things don't go exactly as you'd hoped.

"Surrender is a journey
from the outer turmoil
to the inner peace."

– SRI CHINMOY

"See the light in others
and treat them as if that's
all you see."

– WAYNE W. DYER

SEEK SUPPORT

Don't carry the world on your shoulders and try to do everything
yourself. At work, delegate and seek support from colleagues to
avoid an unnecessary build-up of stress. Engage in teamwork
to relieve the anxiety of feeling like you have sole responsibility
for everything.

"A man of calm is like a shady tree. People who need shelter come to it."

– TOBA BETA

"Peace doesn't mean that you will not have problems. Peace means that your problems will not have you."

– TONY EVANS

"Retain a calm heart, sit like a turtle, walk swiftly like a pigeon, and sleep like a dog."

– LI CHING-YUEN

MOVE YOUR BODY

Exercise releases feel-good endorphins, helps to balance stress hormones, and is an essential component of our overall well-being. Even if you can't fit in regular vigorous workouts, take the stairs instead of the elevator, park further away and walk the last block, dance while you're waiting for the kettle to boil…

"It is easy to have calmness in inactivity, it is hard to have calmness in activity, but calmness in activity is true calmness."

– SHUNRYŪ SUZUKI

TELL THE TRUTH

Being open and honest leads to a calm state of mind. If you have
nothing to hide you will be more at peace with yourself.

"One cool judgment is worth
a thousand hasty counsels.
The thing to do is to supply
light and not heat."

— WOODROW WILSON

KNOW YOUR STRESS TRIGGERS

Look at how you react to tricky situations and ask yourself the reasons why. Understanding what really pushes your buttons and winds you up into a stressed state of mind is the first step in letting it go.

"Anger is an acid that can do more harm to the vessel in which it is stored than anything on which it is poured."

– MARK TWAIN

"Do you have the patience to wait until your mud settles and the water is clear?"

– LAOZI

CHOOSE CALM

You alone are responsible for your own reactions to any situation. You can choose your behavior at any given moment. Mentally prepare yourself for difficult situations and envisage your calm and measured response.

"Beyond drama and chaos, beyond anxiety and fear, lies a zone of endless peace and love. Let's all take a very deep breath, slow down for just a moment and remember this. That alone will open the door."

– MARIANNE WILLIAMSON

"The poor long for riches, the rich long for heaven, but the wise long for a state of tranquility."

– SWAMI RAMA

CLEAR THE CLUTTER

Your home should be your haven, a place where you can escape from the pressures of everyday life. Studies have shown it's much harder to do this when you're surrounded by clutter. So today, set some time aside to clear out those items you no longer want or need and create a calm space you can truly relax in.

"Travel light, live light, spread the light, be the light."

– YOGI BHAJAN

JUNE 7TH

"The thing to do is
to keep your mind when
the world around you
is losing theirs."

– WARREN BUFFETT

USE PMR

Use progressive muscle relaxation (PMR) techniques. This involves lying down with your eyes closed and moving through all the muscle groups in your body, clenching them tight for 5 seconds, then releasing.

"When you find peace within yourself, you become the kind of person who can live at peace with others."

– PEACE PILGRIM

WRAP YOURSELF IN LOVE

Surround yourself with people you love and who love you to achieve inner serenity.

"Compassion automatically brings happiness and calmness. Then, even if you receive disturbing news, it will be easier to take, as your mind is still."

– DALAI LAMA

"Anger is a wind which blows out the lamp of the mind."

– ROBERT GREEN INGERSOLL

COUNT TO 10

Feel the rage brewing, tears prickling the backs of your eyes? Try the old-tech method of counting to 10. Distancing yourself from the situation at hand for this short time will allow you to drop back in with a refreshed, calmer mind.

"Raise your words, not your voice. It is rain that grows flowers, not thunder."

– RUMI

"When you walk in peace you will literally see attackers shattering themselves against your inner-calm. They will defeat themselves."

– BRYANT MCGILL

DRINK YOGI TEA

Soothe your soul with a cup of calming yogi tea.
Boil up together:

1 cup water
2–3 slices of fresh root ginger
½ cinnamon stick
3–4 cloves
3–4 black peppercorns
5–7 green cardamom pods
Black tea, to taste
Milk, to taste
Honey, to taste (optional)

"Like water, we are truest to our nature in repose."

– CYRIL CONNOLLY

"Though I am often in the depths of misery, there is still calmness, pure harmony and music inside me."

— VINCENT VAN GOGH

KNOW YOURSELF

Inner peace will only come with knowledge of your authentic self. Take time to meditate on your values, your passions, your goals…and anything else that defines you as a unique individual.

"There are no better cosmetics than a severe temperance and purity, modesty and humility, a gracious temper and calmness of spirit; and there is no true beauty without the signatures of these graces in the very countenance."

– ARTHUR HELPS

"I am never in a hurry, because I never undertake more work than I can go through with perfect calmness of spirit."

– JOHN WESLEY

LOSE THE ADRENALINE

Try to avoid leading an adrenaline-fuelled lifestyle, which will impact your health and your peace of mind. Slow down and you'll be both healthier and happier.

"The hurrier I go,
the behinder I get."

– LEWIS CARROLL

"When we observe the flow of our breathing, we transcend our thoughts and are able to bring mind and body into harmony with each other. Thus, we create calm."

– CHRISTOPHER DINES

MEDITATE

Find your inner silence through meditation. You don't have to have practiced meditation before—there are many guided meditation apps or YouTube videos available for everyone.

"Meditation is not a way of making your mind quiet. It is a way of entering into the quiet that is already there— buried under the 50,000 thoughts the average person thinks every day."

– DEEPAK CHOPRA

"The music is not in the notes, but in the silence between."

– WOLFGANG AMADEUS MOZART

CHOOSE YOUR WORDS CAREFULLY

Don't let your inner chatter spill out—say nothing unless it's true, kind, or useful.

"If there were a little more silence, if we all kept quiet...maybe we could understand something."

– FEDERICO FELLINI

"If your teeth are clenched and your fists are clenched, your lifespan is probably clenched."

– TERRI GUILLEMETS

"We have forgotten what rocks and plants still know—we have forgotten how to be—to be still—to be ourselves—to be where life is here and now."

– ECKHART TOLLE

"Step outside for a while—
calm your mind. It is
better to hug a tree than to
bang your head against a
wall continually."

– RASHEED OGUNLARU

WALK

Take a 5-minute walk outside, and leave all electronic devices at home or on your desk. Simply listen to your footsteps and observe your surroundings. You will return with a quieter mind.

"Observe the wonders as they occur around you. Don't claim them. Feel the artistry moving through and be silent."

– RUMI

"Without judgment,
we let each thing, event,
day, and feeling be
whatever it is."

– MELODY BEATTIE

ACCEPT YOURSELF

Reframe what you regard as your negative traits into positive ones to help you along the path toward self-acceptance. You will only ever find inner peace if you truly accept yourself for who you are.

"There's calm in the mind of the humble. An unmistakable peace of not having to prove anything to anyone."

– RON BARATONO

CLEANSE YOUR LIFE

Keep your life as simple and honest as possible. Let go of all the people and extraneous material goods that no longer serve you.

"Freedom from desire
leads to inner peace."

– LAOZI

"Finish each day and be done with it. You have done what you could; some blunders and absurdities no doubt crept in; forget them as soon as you can. Tomorrow is a new day; you shall begin it well and serenely and with too high a spirit to be encumbered with your old nonsense."

– RALPH WALDO EMERSON

"Worry pretends to
be necessary, but
serves no useful
purpose."

– ECKHART TOLLE

"The more tranquil a man becomes, the greater is his success, his influence, his power for good. Calmness of mind is one of the beautiful jewels of wisdom."

– JAMES ALLEN

LIVE IN THE MOMENT

Being completely present in the moment will enhance feelings of calm and contentment. Practice a mindfulness meditation to ground yourself in the now. Or simply look out of the window and observe the color of the sky, take a sip of your coffee and notice the sensation as it glides down your throat, feel the warmth of the mug, the feel of your clothes against your skin, the light from the window in the room…

"Yesterday is ashes, tomorrow wood. Only today does the fire burn brightly. Live Today!"

– ESKIMO PROVERB

"Remain calm, serene, always in command of yourself. You will then find out how easy it is to get along."

– PARAMAHANSA YOGANANDA

"There are times in
life when there's
absolutely nothing you
can do, also known as
a chance to relax."

— ROBERT BRAULT

FIND THE FUNNY SIDE

Deliberately look for sources of amusement and joy when times get tough. Everything is more manageable if you can find something to laugh at.

"The pursuit, even of the best things, ought to be calm and tranquil."

– MARCUS TULLIUS CICERO

SET LIMITS

If your life is over-scheduled and over-filled, it's time to start setting limits. Limit unnecessary things such as the number of times you check your phone and the number of non-urgent emails you reply to immediately.

"The superior person
is calm and composed;
the lesser person is
continuously worried
and distressed."

– CONFUCIUS

ESCAPE

You don't need to run for the hills to do this. Simply reading a
good book or watching a favorite movie will allow you to relax and
escape to another world free from the pressures of everyday life.

"Relaxation comes
from letting go of
tense thoughts."

– FRANCES WILSHIRE

RELEASE STRESS

Curse into your pillow, cry if you want to, phone a friend, doodle your way to distraction, or go for a run. Whatever you do, don't keep the feelings locked inside.

"You will find peace not by trying to escape your problems, but by confronting them courageously. You will find peace not in denial but in victory."

– J. DONALD WALTERS

INDULGE IN "ME TIME"

Taking time out for yourself away from the constant demands of your life is essential if you are to achieve a balanced state of mind.

"Calm mind brings inner
strength and self-confidence,
so that's very important
for good health."

– DALAI LAMA

BREATHE FROM YOUR DIAPHRAGM

When anxious or stressed our breathing tends to be quick and shallow. Combat this by breathing deeply into your diaphragm. Check your breathing by placing one hand on your chest and the other on your lower abdomen. As you inhale, you should feel your belly rise.

"Peace begins from within, if you are not peaceful inside, the world will be chaotic."

– UNKNOWN

"The chaos doesn't end,
you kinda' just become
the calm."

– NIKKI ROWE

"Nothing can bring you peace but yourself."

– RALPH WALDO EMERSON

"Ego says, 'Once everything falls into place, I'll feel peace.' Spirit says, 'Find your peace, and then everything will fall into place.'"

– MARIANNE WILLIAMSON

"The simplification of life is one of the steps to inner peace. A persistent simplification will create an inner and outer well-being that places harmony in one's life."

– PEACE PILGRIM

"Tension is who you think you should be. Relaxation is who you are."

– CHINESE PROVERB

ONE THING AT A TIME

Multitasking leads to a chaotic mindset and little productivity.
Focus on one thing at a time and you are far
more likely to calmly and steadfastly achieve each goal.

"You have to slow your heart rate, stay calm. You have to shoot in between your heartbeats."

– CHRIS KYLE

"The day she let go of the things that were weighing her down was the day she began to shine the brightest."

– KATRINA MAYER

BE POSITIVE

Maintain a positive outlook and your path to inner peace will be a far less rocky one. The more we are able to look on the bright side, the better we are able to deal calmly with stressful situations that are beyond our control.

"When the odds are hopeless,
when all seems to be lost, then
is the time to be calm."

– IAN FLEMING

"How beautiful it is
to be alive!"

– HENRY S. SUTTON

"Just remember, the storm doesn't last forever. It can scare you; it can shake you to your core. But it never lasts. The rain subsides, the thunder dies, and the winds calm to a soft whisper. And that moment after the storm clouds pass, when all is silent and still, you find peace. Quiet, gentle peace."

– S.L. JENNINGS

"Peace doesn't deny difficulty, but it has an inner calm and quietness even while enduring the difficulty."

– GLENN C. STEWART

FROM MIND TO BODY

To achieve calm in moments of stress, switch your focus
from your mind to your body. Instead of replaying a frustrating
situation over and over in your head, focus instead on
your body using the below exercise:

1. Find a quiet place to sit and simply notice the feel of the
chair beneath you.

2. Sit up tall and relax your shoulders, and try to bring your
shoulder blades together.

3. Inhale through your nose for a count of four, hold for two,
and exhale through your mouth for seven.

4. Repeat this cycle at least five times.

This will calm your chattering mind, just as the depth of breath
will calm your nervous system.

"If you get the inside right,
the rest will fall into place."

– ECKHART TOLLE

"The quieter you become the more you can hear."

– UNKNOWN

PRACTICE TAI CHI

Tai chi's focus on deep breathing, meditation, and gentle flowing movements is a wonderful calming tool.

"Everything we do is infused with the energy with which we do it. If we're frantic, life will be frantic. If we're peaceful, life will be peaceful."

— MARIANNE WILLIAMSON

EAT WELL

In times of stress it's natural to want to reach for cake or other sugary treats for instant comfort. However, the sharp spike in your blood sugar levels is only going to make you feel more jittery. Making healthier snack choices can actually reduce stress—research suggests, for example, that the vitamin C in fruits decreases stress-induced free radicals. Also try making your meals from scratch using nutritional whole foods and enjoy the meditative process that cooking can be.

"A crust eaten in peace
is better than a banquet
partaken in anxiety."

– AESOP

BRING THE OUTSIDE IN

Potted plants and flowers are a great way to bring nature into your home. Having flowers and plants nearby will calm an anxious mind.

"Adopt the pace of nature:
her secret is patience."

– RALPH WALDO EMERSON

"Bloom where you are planted."

– UNKNOWN

FIND STILLNESS

Take a few moments every day to simply sit still
doing absolutely nothing.

"Silence is the sleep that nourishes wisdom."

– FRANCIS BACON

"Holding on to anger is like grasping a hot coal with the intent of throwing it at someone else; you are the one who gets burned."

– BUDDHA

FORGIVE

Forgive yourself first and then you will find it easier to forgive others. You cannot achieve inner peace if you are harboring resentments. When you forgive, you set yourself free from negative thought patterns that impede your ability to find peace.

"Inner peace begins the moment you choose not to allow another person or event to control your emotions."

– PEMA CHÖDRÖN

"Anger dwells only in the
bosom of fools."

– ALBERT EINSTEIN

BECOME YOUR OWN BEST FRIEND

Stop seeking from others what you can find within yourself.
Become your own support system.

"When we are unable to find tranquility within ourselves, it is useless to seek it elsewhere."

– FRANÇOIS DE LA ROCHEFOUCAULD

WRITE IT DOWN

Get whatever is bothering you down on paper. This cathartic process of writing about your frustrations will really help to clear your mind.

"If you kick a stone
in anger you will hurt
your foot."

– KOREAN PROVERB

"Tranquil as a forest, but on fire within, once you find your center, you are sure to win."

– DAVID ZIPPEL

"You have power over your mind—not outside events. Realize this, and you will find strength."

– MARCUS AURELIUS

"Between stimulus
and response, there is
a space. In that space
is our power to choose
our response. In our
response lies our growth
and our freedom."

– VIKTOR FRANKL

LET GO OF THE NEED TO BE LIKED BY EVERYONE

When you focus too much on making people like you, you will lose sight of your authentic self. Stop being a people-pleaser and accept that you will never be everyone's favorite person.

"Peace is the result of retraining your mind to process life as it is, rather than as you think it should be."

– WAYNE W. DYER

WRITE AFFIRMATIONS

Write a list of anchoring words or phrases that help you to feel calm, such as "Everything is as it should be," "I am at peace with my life," or "My worries are floating away on a gentle breeze." Repeat these affirmations whenever you need to return to a sense of serenity.

"When everything
around you is crazy,
it is ingenious
to stay calm."

– MEHMET MURAT ILDAN

HUG A TREE

Many tree species are believed to have a specific calming effect on both the mind and body. Pick a tree that appeals to you and hug it, or sit against its trunk for a few moments, absorbing its calming energy.

"To sit in the shade on a fine day and look upon verdure is the most perfect refreshment."

– JANE AUSTEN

"The key to a calm mind is to spend some time with oneself."

– ASHUTOSH MISHRA

STREAMLINE YOUR DIARY

Cut out all unnecessary obligations and learn how to say no!

"To find peace, sometimes you have to be willing to lose your connection with the people, places, and things that create all the noise in your life."

– UNKNOWN

"Vows made in storms
are forgotten in calm."

– THOMAS FULLER

ASSERT YOURSELF

If you become too passive or submissive, you will end up carrying a lot of pent up frustrations. Learn to assert yourself and find solutions that won't leave you feeling wronged.

"Obstacles do not block the path, they are the path."

– ZEN PROVERB

"Tranquility is nothing
else than the good ordering
of the mind."

– MARCUS AURELIUS

SLEEP

Go to bed earlier to ensure you get a full eight hours of sleep.
When we're frazzled and grumpy life does not go smoothly!
Studies have shown that even minor sleep disturbances can
impact on our memory, concentration, and mood.

"Clarity Brings Serenity."

– TEODOMILA

TRY AROMATHERAPY

Add a few drops of relaxing essential oils to your bath, or
massage them into your feet for an instant soothing effect.

"Each one has to find his peace from within. And peace to be real must be unaffected by outside circumstances."

– MAHATMA GANDHI

"Peace is a condition of the heart. It's a state of mind, of tranquility, of calmness, and of centeredness."

– DENNIS KUCINICH

SELECT A CENTERING OBJECT

Choose an object such as a smooth pebble you can keep in your pocket, or a locket around your neck. Touch this object whenever you're feeling stressed or anxious to center you and help calm your thoughts.

SEPTEMBER 22ND

"Calmness is the graceful
form of confidence."

– MARIE VON EBNER-ESCHENBACH

"Those who tried to break you are expecting you to be in fight mode. Conquer them with your peace."

– THEMA DAVIS

LEARN TO LOVE YOUR ENEMY

Harboring resentments toward perceived enemies is really going to kill your calm. Visualize your enemy as a much-loved friend or family member and you should find yourself feeling gentler thoughts toward them next time you are in their company.

"When anger rises, think of the consequences."

– CONFUCIUS

"Simply let experience take place very freely, so that your open heart is suffused with the tenderness of true compassion."

– TSOKNYI RINPOCHE

"Don't rush anything.
When the time is right,
it'll happen."

– UNKNOWN

WALK DON'T RUN

To the shops, to meetings, to pick up children from school, to meet friends…wherever you're heading walk, don't run. Leave plenty of time and make your way to appointments with a gentle ease.

"Patience is a
form of wisdom."

– JON KABAT-ZINN

"Excitement is not enjoyment: in calmness lies true pleasure. The most precious wines are sipped, not bolted at a swallow."

– VICTOR HUGO

"The quiet mind is richer than a crown."

– ROBERT GREENE

"You cannot perceive beauty, but with a serene mind."

– HENRY DAVID THOREAU

PLAN TO BE CALM

While we can never know the exact outcome of any given situation, we can make sensible predictions. If you have a potentially stressful situation on the horizon, consider all the possible outcomes and plan your reaction to each of these ahead of time. It is much easier to stay calm if you've already acted out doing just that in your head.

"Patience is not the ability to wait. Patience is to be calm no matter what happens, constantly take action to turn it to positive growth opportunities, and have faith to believe that it will all work out in the end while you are waiting."

– ROY T. BENNETT

"Worry is as useless as a handle on a snowball."

– MITZI CHANDLER

"If you're going to live in the anxiety of the surface of this world, you're never going to find the depth, the source. If you want calmness, you've got to go deeper."

– AGAPI STASSINOPOULOS

"Music comes from an icicle
as it melts, to live again as
spring water."

– HENRY WILLIAMSON

LISTEN TO
CALMING MUSIC

Take a few moments out of a busy day to let your favorite
calming melodies wash over you. The instant soothing effect
is evidence this is medicine for your soul.

"Nature does not hurry but yet everything is accomplished."

– LAOZI

SLOWLY, SLOWLY...

Living each moment rushing to get to the next is a surefire way to increase tension throughout the body and mind. You may feel as though you have no choice but to rush, but there is always an option to slow down. In fact, everything will improve if you do— your work, your health, and your state of mind.

"Dripping water hollows out stone, not through force but through persistence."

– OVID

"The day you stop racing, is the day you win the race."

– BOB MARLEY

"Let them come, let
them be, let them go."

– CULADASA

KNOW YOUR STRESS SIGNS

Knowing how your body reacts to stress can help prevent it creeping up on you. Writing a list of your signs of stress— irritability, tearfulness, lack of focus and concentration, anger, or frustration...can help you become more aware and therefore more able to manage it.

"Let everything happen
to you: beauty and terror.
Just keep going. No feeling
is final."

– RAINER MARIA RILKE

SING YOUR HEART OUT

Singing has been proven to release feel-good hormones that reduce stress and anxiety. Consider joining a choir for the added benefit of human connectivity—studies have shown that choristers' heartbeats synchronize when they sing together, bringing about a communal calming effect.

"Quiet the mind and the
soul will speak."

– MA JAYA SATI BHAGAVATI

TAKE A HOT BATH

As the heat relaxes your muscles and eases any aches and pains, then so your mind relaxes. For added calm, add candles and a rose-scented bath oil.

"There must be quite a few things that a hot bath won't cure, but I don't know many of them."

– SYLVIA PLATH

"I've begun to realize that you can listen to silence and learn from it. It has a quality and a dimension all its own."

– CHAIM POTOK

LAY YOUR HEAD ON A PILLOW

While your day may not allow time out for a nap, you can always take just a minute or two to reset. Lay your head on a pillow and visualize all your worries and stresses soaking into the pillow as if it were a sponge. After a couple of minutes, raise your head feeling calmer and rejuvenated.

"A ruffled mind makes
a restless pillow."

– CHARLOTTE BRONTË

"Do your work, then step back. The only path to serenity."

– LAOZI

SMELL THE ROSES

The soothing scents of flowers can stimulate smell receptors in the nose that connect to the part of the brain that regulates emotions. So next time you're feeling overwhelmed by stress, take some time out to smell the roses.

"No peace lies in the future which is not hidden in this present little instant."

– ANNE LAMOTT

"Opportunity seldom rises with blood pressure."

– JAROD KINTZ

STRETCH

Stretching your muscles relaxes your body, which in turn relaxes your mind.

"A heart at peace gives
life to the body."

– UNKNOWN

SOCIALIZE

Socializing is a great stress reliever. Spend time with groups of good friends and the interaction will help you to unwind effortlessly.

"Choose your thoughts carefully. Keep what brings you peace, release what brings you suffering, and know that happiness is just a thought away."

– NISHAN PANWAR

"Many a calm river begins as
a turbulent waterfall, yet none
hurtles and foams all the way
to the sea."

– MIKHAIL LERMONTOV

"Deep down, nature is inherently peaceful, calm, and beautiful. The universe as a whole is perfect. The chaos is on the surface."

– AMIT RAY

"Keep calm and
keep learning."

– LAILAH GIFTY AKITA

LISTEN TO YOURSELF

If you find yourself losing your patience easily and you're having more trouble than usual staying calm, it's time to take a step back and ask yourself why. Are you working too long hours without a break? Not taking enough time out for self-care? Schedule in more time to do the things that relax you and bring you back to your self.

"In silence there
is eloquence. Stop
weaving and see how
the pattern improves."

– RUMI

TURN THE VOLUME DOWN

Don't be afraid of silence. Turn off the TV and radio, shut down your computer, switch your cell phone to silent, and let your mind wander in the stillness. Carve out time for this quiet contemplation.

"Let peace be your
middle name."

– NTATHU ALLEN

"If a person's basic state of mind is serene and calm, then it is possible for this inner peace to overwhelm a painful physical experience."

– DALAI LAMA

CONNECT

If you can truly connect with your self—through meditation, breathing techniques, yoga, or another form of self-care—you will be able to carry your inner calm into even the most hectic of environments.

"Ships don't sink because of the water around them. They sink because of the water that gets in them."

– UNKNOWN

"Saying nothing
sometimes says
the most."

– EMILY DICKINSON

DITCH THE DRAMA

Anyone who generates drama in your life is having a negative impact. Engage instead in harmonious relationships with people who enhance your sense of well-being.

"Inner peace can be reached only when we practice forgiveness. Forgiveness is letting go of the past, and is therefore the means for correcting our misperceptions."

– GERALD G. JAMPOLSKY

"The fruit of silence is tranquility."

– ARABIAN PROVERB

TRY TRANSCENDENTAL MEDITATION

This meditation technique involves sitting in silence for 20 minutes or more and repeating a mantra. It's wonderful for quieting a chattering mind and achieving true stillness.

1. Close your eyes and bring your mantra to mind.

2. As your mind wanders become aware that you are no longer hearing your mantra. This awareness alone will enable you to return effortlessly to it.

3. Toward the end of meditation bring your attention back to your body and the room you are in for a few minutes before opening your eyes.

"Nowhere can man find a quieter or more untroubled retreat than in his own soul."

– MARCUS AURELIUS

"Do you want to
change yourself?
Then remain
completely silent inside
the silence-sea."

– SRI CHINMOY

DIRECT YOUR ENERGIES WISELY

Are you in the wrong job or surrounded by friends who drain you? Invest your time in people and things that speak to your heart and calm your mind.

"Only one-fourth of the sorrow in each man's life is caused by outside uncontrollable elements, the rest is self-imposed by failing to analyze and act with calmness."

– HOLBROOK JACKSON

"Patience is seeing each step as a journey rather than seeing a journey as a thousand steps."

– RICHELLE E. GOODRICH

BE REALISTIC

If you are finding yourself stressed and overwhelmed, are you being realistic in what you can achieve? Reset your goals so they are attainable and stop reaching for unrealistic standards that will leave you feeling as though you're always running to catch up.

NOVEMBER 21ST

"To increase speed you
must increase the amount
of rest, peace, calmness
that you can maintain.
That is the secret to
playing fast."

– PEPE ROMERO

DANCE

If you don't have the time or the inclination to attend regular dance classes, simply bust your moves on the kitchen (dance) floor. Dancing to your favorite tunes will release mood-boosting endorphins and ease any pent-up tension.

"I crowded far too many tasks into Yesterday. Today is now demanding music, chocolate truffles, and sporadic dancing, as compensation."

– DR. SUNWOLF

"The soul becomes
dyed with the color
of its thoughts."

– MARCUS AURELIUS

STOP PROCRASTINATING

Put effort into solving problems that are weighing heavy on your mind. More often than not, you'll know exactly what needs doing to resolve these niggles but spend too long procrastinating over them.

"Don't let your mind bully your body into believing it must carry the burden of its worries."

– TERRI GUILLEMETS

GIVE UP CONTROL

It's time to let go of any control-freak tendencies if you want to achieve true inner harmony. Let go of those situations and people you cannot control. In any situation ask yourself "What can I do about this?" If it can't be changed, accept it and move on.

"Acceptance of others, their looks, their behaviors, their beliefs, brings you an inner peace and tranquility—instead of anger and resentment."

– UNKNOWN

"Deep below the shimmering surface lies a vast reservoir of awareness, sometimes forgotten, but always there."

– TAMARA LEVITT

"Feelings are just visitors, let them come and go."

– MOOJI

"The only order in the universe is just a cycle of calm and chaos."

– TOBA BETA

LOOSEN UP

Scan your body to find areas of tension. Unclench your jaw, relax your shoulders, do neck rolls, circle your wrists, or flex your feet to encourage relaxation of any tense muscles.

"Understand this and be free:
we are not in our bodies; our
bodies are inside us."

– SEAN A. MULVIHILL

"Some of the secret joys of living are not found by rushing from point A to point B, but by inventing some imaginary letters along the way."

– DOUGLAS PAGELS

TIMELESS CHALLENGE

Leave your watch at home and challenge yourself for one day to
forget what time it is.

"Indeed, there will
be time…"

– T.S. ELIOT

"The two most powerful
warriors are patience
and time."

– LEO TOLSTOY

"Our peace shall stand as firm as rocky mountains."

– WILLIAM SHAKESPEARE

MEDITATE ON ART

Pick a piece of art such as a painting and set aside 5 minutes to meditate on it. How does it make you feel? What do you observe as you look further into the artwork? What details can you now see that you missed at first glance? What story arises in your mind as you view the art?...

"Don't underestimate the value of Doing Nothing, of just going along, listening to all the things you can't hear, and not bothering."

– A.A. MILNE

"Peace cannot be kept by force; it can only be achieved by understanding."

– ALBERT EINSTEIN

QUESTION YOUR THOUGHTS

Try to become aware of your thoughts and you will start to notice when you fall into negative patterns of thinking that disrupt your inner peace. The more attuned you become to your mind's natural rhythm, the more you'll be able to control your thought processes.

"Do not anticipate trouble or worry about what may never happen. Keep in the sunlight."

– BENJAMIN FRANKLIN

"The best thing one can do when it is raining is let it rain."

– HENRY WADSWORTH LONGFELLOW

EXPRESS YOURSELF

Nobody can read your mind, so when situations frustrate you, speak out. Learn to communicate effectively and avoid the build-up of futile resentments that will stand in the way of inner peace.

"Do not learn how to react.
Learn how to respond."

– BUDDHA

PRACTICE A LITTLE ACUPRESSURE

Going for a massage is not always an option, but you can easily and quickly practice techniques such as acupressure on yourself. Try pressing your thumb on the point where the inside of your wrist forms a crease with your hand for two minutes to release tension.

"Everything you do can
be done better from a
place of relaxation."

– STEPHEN C. PAUL

"On even the most
stressful days, magic is
still sitting quietly in the
corner, waiting to
be noticed."

– DR. SUNWOLF

CULTIVATE ROUTINE

Get routines in place and much of the daily grind will simply
fall into place.

"Slow down and everything you are chasing will come around and catch you."

– JOHN DE PAOLA

ASK FOR HELP

Use your support system of friends or family when you're in need. Trying to take on the world and do everything solo will lead to a state of constant stress and worry.

"Stress is an ignorant
state. It believes
that everything is
an emergency."

– NATALIE GOLDBERG

"Seek not that the things which happen should happen as you wish; but wish the things which happen to be as they are, and you will have a tranquil flow of life."

– EPICTETUS

"Find your center
and live in it."

– RALPH WALDO TRINE

CLOSE YOUR EYES

This is such a simple technique to regain inner calm and composure—block out the world for a few seconds just by lowering your eyelids.

"Can we get to the place where there is no place to get to?"

– MICHAEL STONE

"How beautiful it is to do nothing, and then to rest afterward."

– SPANISH PROVERB

PRIORITIZE PEACE

Will you look back on your life and wish you had rushed about more in a frazzled manner, or will you celebrate the moments of calm and connectedness; relationships and experiences that you fully embraced and enjoyed in the moment?

DECEMBER 30TH

"Life is like the ocean, it can
be calm or still, and rough
or rigid, but in the end, it is
always beautiful."

– UNKNOWN

"When you realize how perfect everything is you will tilt your head back and laugh at the sky."

– BUDDHA